Dennis —

Keep the fire
a-glow!

Susan Carol Hauser
1/14/2010

Sugartime

Sugartime

The Hidden Pleasures of Making Maple Syrup
with a Primer for the Novice Sugarer

SUSAN CAROL HAUSER

THE LYONS PRESS

Design by Catherine Lau Hunt
Section illustrations by Joan Nygren
Photographs by Susan Hauser, unless otherwise noted
Frontispiece by Michael DeWitt
10 9 8 7 6 5 4 3 2 1

PERMISSIONS
Grateful acknowledgment is made to the following for
permission to reprint material:
University of Minnesota Press, for portions of *Sugartime*
previously published in *North Writers II*, 1997.
Minnesota Monthly for recipes.
For photographs: William H. McDowall; Vivienne
Morgan; Tamara Wentworth; Beltrami County Historical
Society, Bemidji, Minnesota.
For artwork: Michael DeWitt; Joan Nygren; the family of
Terri Anderson; *Minnesota Calls* magazine.

Library of Congress Cataloging-in-Publication Data

Hauser, Susan, 1942–
    Sugartime: the hidden pleasures of making maple syrup
    with a primer for the novice sugarer / Susan Carol Hauser.
        p.   cm.
    Includes bibliographical references.
    ISBN 1-55821-599-9
    1. Maple sugar. 2. Maple syrup. I. Title.
TP395.H38   1997
664'.132—dc21   97-6630
                                                      CIP

This kettle song is for Bill; and for Chery, Joel, and Sean;
Kathy, Scott, and Chabin; and Barbara, Myron, Kael,
and
Dustin, who also keep the fire aglow.

MY THANKS

To Earl Nyholm for the story of *anininaatig,* the sacred maple; and to Robert, Carmen, and Douglas Maschler, and Rolland and Jenny Warner for their stories.

To Hilda Rachuy; Mary, Andy, Sonya, and Danny Clemenson; Rose and Will Weaver; Vivienne and Michael Morgan; and Chabin Blanc for joining Bill and me in the circle of the trees.

To Martha Dunaway for her maple recipes.

To Vern Holzhueter, for paying attention.

To Dave and Tamara Wentworth for their knowledge of the finer points of sugaring.

To Brian Donovan, who honors language.

To Helen Bonner, my faithful reader.

To Lilly Golden for her patience, grace, and editorial wisdom.

Contents

Foreword

"IMPATIENCE IS OUR NIGHTMARE," the poet Philip Levine has written. He was referring to the ever-accelerating pace of modern life and its great pains upon our spirit; in particular he suggests that we have lost our ability to work quietly, steadily within the embrace of our work and with faith in the eventual pleasure of completion. Franz Kafka, too, had his complaints in the area. For humankind, he wrote, ". . . perhaps there is only one major sin: impatience. Because of impatience they were expelled (from paradise), because of impatience they do not return."

Impatience. No one is immune. However, to read Susan Carol Hauser's *Sugartime* is to return to the one small paradise available to everyone: the slow pleasures of good work.

Let me explain what I mean by "good work." A few years ago, as my contribution to a friend's wedding day, I volunteered to roast a pig. It had been years since I had done this sort of thing, and of course it quickly became far more labor than I remembered. With ten minutes and fifty dollars I could have gone to the meat market and bought a wedding ham that would have made Charles Dickens proud, but no, here I was, the night before the wedding, stuck turning a hog on a hot iron spit while everyone else went off to dance. Resignedly I tended to my work. By ten p.m. I was irritable; by eleven o'clock, tormented; by midnight, exhausted. At one a.m. the partiers came back and gathered boisterously around the fire; their company lifted my spirits, but the dancers were danced out and soon enough straggled off to bed, leaving me alone, again, with my fire and my hog. Throughout the night I kept the coals cherry red and the meat cooking, an interminable night—until, slowly, like a tide of moonlight or a change in the weather, something magical happened. In the steady rhythms of the fire, in the continual hiss and snap of grease falling on red coals, in the gradual slowing down of my life, I began to wake up. I woke up from one kind of work, one kind of time, one kind of life, and crossed into another. It was four a.m., not a car on the street, nighthawks gone back to their nests and the earliest birds still dozing in the darkest hour before dawn, but I was happily, joyously wide awake: I had stumbled upon good work, the kind that slows time and deepens the spirit.

Maple sugaring, it seems clear to me from reading *Sugartime,* is a similarly good kind of work. Maple sugaring will not be hurried. It is more than the work of one night or one week; its rhythms are measured in sunlight and shadow, in the tilt of the earth's axis and in the ancient memories of trees.

There is much work and there is much waiting: waiting for the late-winter snow to loosen its grip on the necks of the sugar maple trees; working to hammer in the taps, to hang the buckets and then wait again. When the temperature eases up to forty-five degrees, Susan Carol Hauser writes, "Anticipation is rewarded . . . a drop of sap quivers on the lip of the spile . . . I watch the clear bead gather strength and let go, . . . as another takes its place." Now the real labor begins. Frosty nights and sunny days make the sap come faster; daily there is the gathering of the pails, daily the tending of fire as the great iron kettle simmers and sings. Daily, patiently, this work in the mud and the heat until the earth itself calls a halt: the season is over. What remains are the glowing jars of syrup and, luckily for us, this fine book.

Will Weaver, Bemidji, Minnesota, Spring 1997
Gravestone Made of Wheat
Farm Team

Section 1

Sugartime

IN NORTHERN MINNESOTA, in late March or early April, the ice is still on the lakes, and snow is still on the ground. But below the earth's surface, seasonal warming has begun and sap starts its journey up into the trees. We know this is happening because of the birds that return, first the bald eagles, then flickers and robins, and we know it because for seven previous winters we have sugared and I have kept a daily journal of dates and temperatures, of gallons of sap and pints of syrup.

This year on March fifth, after several days of forty degree temps, we trudged out to the storage shed and retrieved our sugaring equipment: electric drill, aluminum taps—called spiles—pails and liners, and hammer. We plodded through the knee-deep snow to the four nearest maple trees and drilled into the frozen wood. Three of the four started dripping when we pulled the drill from the hole. We hung pails lined with plastic sugaring sacks, even though we knew it was too early for a good sap run. For the next two weeks the temperature stuck at thirty degrees and the three cooperating trees yielded up only a few quarts of sap, far less than the average one-half to one gallon a day per tree we could hope for later on.

Almost every year we tease ourselves into the same premature behavior, eager for this special time to begin, and betraying our contemporary attitude. Until the middle of this century, for the Ojibwe people, sugaring was one point in the cycle of seasons. Just before the month of the Sugar Moon they moved from their winter camp to the sugarbush. Later they moved on to their gardening and berry summer camps, then to the fall and winter hunting camps. Sugaring was part of the circle.

For us, for my husband, Bill, and me, sugaring is a step out of the circle. For several weeks in the months of March and April we give up the clock and the calendar that guide us through the weekdays and weekends, daytimes and evenings of the rest of the year. We are led instead by the flow of the sap, which rises and falls to the whim of the temperature.

By March we are ready to give up our meticulous winter routine. We eat by the clock because daylight fails us. During the week we work days and sit quietly at night, as though if we moved about too much we might break something cosmic made brittle by the cold. On the weekends we do chores in preparation for the week.

The trees do not mind our eagerness to join their party, even when we attempt to preempt the season by a few weeks. The taps just sit there, dry if the tree chooses, or damp with maybe a drop or two if the sap is stirring. Most years we are ahead of ourselves by at least a week.

This year on March eighteenth I stop, as usual, on my way to the mailbox and check the four test trees. It is a warm day, the temperature easing up to forty-five degrees. I am expectant, and my anticipation is rewarded. The spiles of the three trees that released sap sparingly since we tapped them now drip steadily, and a drop of sap quivers on the lip of the spile on the fourth tree, the one that remained dry for the last two weeks. I watch the clear bead gather strength and let go, and continue to watch as another takes its place. Then I resume my trek to the mailbox, smiling all the way there and back, eager to return to the house with the news: Sugartime has begun.

Before we head out to tap trees, we sit a moment at the kitchen table. Tapping is the most strenuous sugaring task. We learned that the first year when we tried to drill our holes with a hand drill. Bill pushed the bit through the rough bark, set it tight against wood, leaned into it and twirled the crankshaft. And twirled the crankshaft. Leaned in harder, and twirled the crank shaft. He stopped, pulled the bit away from the tree, and stared at the little white dot he had made on the frozen trunk.

He looked at me, and I looked at the dot and back at him. We knew that the settlers used hand drills. Later we found out they used something called a breast drill. The end opposite the bit had a flat plate that you leaned into with your chest. And later we realized that they did aerobic activities about twelve hours of every day. The Indians used a blade to cut into the wood, and most of their life was exercise.

"Power?" I said. And side by side we headed for the garage where we found the electric drill and scrounged up outdoor power cords.

Later we bought more extension cords, and today Bill slings coiled heaps of bright orange cords over his shoulder while I check my handbasket for spiles, hammer, and plastic liners, and load the garden cart with five-gallon plastic pails. They are stacked three to a bunch in plastic leaf bags, where I put them last spring after washing them and drying them in the sun.

Together we embark on our pilgrimage to the trees. In other years we have trucked through three feet of snow with our paraphernalia, but this year the ground is mostly bare, although it is also still mostly frozen. Mud slicks, ice slicks, snow patches, and mulching leaves form a slippery, uneven quilt punctuated with fallen branches and sticks, and we watch our feet as we walk.

Like the women and men of the Ojibwe people, Bill and I have certain tasks that we traditionally do. Bill drills holes and, with light strokes of the hammer, taps in the spiles. I hang buckets, and insert and adjust the liners. Bill makes the fire; I check the buckets for sap. We both "pick" in the afternoon, and we both keep the fire going during the day. Late in the afternoon when the sap is close to becoming syrup, I bring the house pan out to the kettle and Bill scoops the sap into it. In the house, I finish off, and Bill helps with the sealing of the jars.

We both participate in choosing the tap site. Today, Bill leading and stringing out power cord while I tug the garden cart over the rough ground, we make our way to the two untapped maples on the north side of the driveway. We stop on the south side of the big maple near the garage. It is a "good" one, always producing some sap, and sometimes producing a lot. As with the other trees, we recognize its personality. It doesn't seem to care where we put the tap, and it's not overly fussy about the weather.

Following sugaring lore, we choose the south side of the tree, which is warmed early by direct sun. Science says it doesn't help, but we still do it if we can find a right spot, one not too close to previous taps, away from boles, and above a good root or below a good branch, where we can be more certain that there is a strong sap channel.

Bill drills the hole and hammers in the tap, and we wait to see if sap will make its way quickly to air. If it does we ooh and ahh appropriately, confirmed in our wisdom. If it does not, we harrumph, and look up and down the tree trunk to see if we have misread it. Either way, Bill then goes ahead to the next maple, finessing the power cord around weeds and deadfall and other trees. I stay to hang the pail, finessing the top flaps of the plastic liner up and around the tap in a sort of tent, and tucking the loose ends under the wire bail of the bucket, so rain, snow, and bugs cannot contaminate the sap.

We move this way from tree to tree, at first gossiping about each one's history, and disagreeing about the best location for this year's tap. But by the time we get to the last trees we are mostly quiet. We listen to the sound of our feet in the wet soil, the squooshing suck of rubber pulling away from mud, and we listen to the birds that watch us, chickadees from near branches, jays from farther off, both gossiping in their bird way about those humans.

When we finish, we have added fourteen taps to the four we did earlier, leaving the two south of the house for another day. About half are already running. Twenty trees should give us eight to fifteen gallons of sap for each day the sap runs. That is enough for us. We can boil off a day's run in one day. On our way back to the house we stop at the kettle, lift off the sheet-metal lid we use to keep out the bits of bark and seed and dust that always float around in a sugarbush, wonder where we left the ladle last year, and then happily though reluctantly slosh our way to the house. We need to sit down. We are weary.

But again we are impatient. We have started something, and we want to stay with it. It is like being packed for a trip, ready to go, but the plane doesn't leave until the next day. Back in the kitchen I content myself with further preparations. I lift the white cloth covering a basket of clean glass jars and look at them, as though they might have changed since I washed them a few days ago. Then I get out my sugaring journal and continue with this year's entry: "Today we tapped fourteen more trees. Eighteen in all. Two to go."

Kettle Song

"WHEN THE KETTLE SINGS, the sap is getting ready to boil."

Bill leans over the kettle as he speaks, and I lean over it, too, and we watch the maple sap we gathered from our trees. Scuzzy beige bubbles scurry around the surface as heat from the wood fire penetrates the heavy cast-iron pot. It looks more like dirty dishwater than potential syrup, but it does sing, an elongated *sssssssssssssss,* the breaking of cold sap against hot iron amplified by the chamber of the kettle, the *akik.*

Akik is the Ojibwe word for "trade kettle." And trade kettle is the name given to the massive cast-iron pots brought here in the nineteenth century by white explorers and traded to American Indians for furs and maple sugar. The *akik* made a difference in the life of the Indian people and so, as with other important objects, it was given an "animate" name and is still today spoken of and treated as though it is a person.

Before the *akik,* maple sap was cooked in birch bark pots. The wet sap kept the bark from burning. Care was taken to keep the pots a distance from flames, but sap does not have to boil to separate sugar from water. It only needs warmth and time, and in the days of the birch bark pots, there was time to let water evaporate.

Today even a trade kettle is too slow for serious sugar makers. The sap is reduced now in long, shallow stainless steel evaporating pans that are heated with wood or fuel oil. Bill and I are dilettantes, serious only about turning ourselves over to the languorous whims of sugartime, and sugaring weather.

Weather is the pump that drives the sap. Even scientists do not yet fully understand the mechanisms of the flow of fluid in trees. Maples and their tribal relatives, box elder and birch, begin to wake up from winter several weeks sooner than the other trees. Because of the way their circulatory systems work, when the temperature is below freezing at night and above forty during the day the sap will flow not only up, but out, if given the opportunity.

There is no compelling mystery to the discovery of the secret of the maple tree. A broken twig will drip sap. As the weather thaws and freezes, sweet icicles form. Squirrels nibble on them, and birds drink their droplets. Children seem to eat them instinctively. And if one lived in the forest, and the winter's snow was gone, and the river was a distance away, it would be easy to break a maple limb and in a few hours catch enough sap for drinking and cooking. And even in a time when there was time, it would be easy to forget the fire for a moment and come back to find a pot of tea turned to maple candy.

Well, that's what happened to our first batch. Maple syrup has its own methodology and is religious about sticking to it. It has taught us diligence,

and we have even become a bit religious about sugartime. We plan no other activities. Our days are
determined by the chant of the thermometer and the
litany of dripping spiles. Our nights are graced with
deep and redemptive sleep.

Our sixty-gallon *akik* is thirty inches in diameter, thirty inches deep, and about nine feet in cir-
cumference. It stands eighteen inches off the
ground, perched on three upright tire rims weld-
ed onto a circle of iron. We bought it at a garage
sale. It almost broke the spirit of our compact sta-
tion wagon when we brought it home, and it
almost broke three human backs getting it onto its
stand. The first year we sugared, we had it near the
back door, because we thought that would be convenient, but the next year we wrestled it again and
put it at the edge of our sugarbush, and now it is
convenient.

Our sugarbush used to consist of twenty-three
mature maples. Two that we used to tap are gone,
lost to storms and since burned in the woodstove

that keeps us warm all winter, and one is a bit too far away for convenience. That leaves us with twenty, and some of those are getting weary. One lost most of its crown in a storm a few years ago. Several have lost branches, and two this year so far refuse to give up a single drop of their sap.

We have more maples on our forty acres, but we use the ones that are handiest. Three are on the north side of the driveway, the rest scattered through the grove due east of the house. The dog yard is also east of the house and in the first days of sugaring our three Saluki hounds pace their forty-by-sixty-foot daytime habitat and wonder what is wrong with us that we are hanging around outside for hours. They watch with some concern as we tromp through snow and slush, kneel in mud to coax the fire, subject our eyes and lungs to heavy smoke, and chill our finger bones in near-freezing sap. We ourselves wonder what human desire has brought us out of the warmth of our house and into this cold kitchen.

Sugarbush Kitchen

FROM THE EAST LIVING-room window I can see most of the sugarbush and the sugaring kettle. The pails hang obediently even in the bit of wind stirring this noon and, this second day after tapping, Bill is working to get the first fire of the season under way. He has shoveled some leftover snow away from the fire pit, adjusted the metal skirt that encircles the lower half of the kettle and the stand, and is now gathering handfuls of little twigs from one of the three woodpiles we put up last summer and covered with tarps.

The ground under the kettle is both wet and icy. Bill puts down a single layer of birch bark, a thick layer of tiny twigs, and tops them with a double layer of slightly larger twigs and branches. He lights the birch bark and when the twigs are burning brightly he adds more, and then more small branches, and keeps doing this until the ground is warm, and the twigs have become ashes, and the small branches have become coals, and gradually he adds larger branches, and finally small logs. He has been bending down into the smoke and the heat for almost an hour.

I join him. The sap in the kettle, about five gallons—half of what we'll start with when the run gets up to speed—has begun to stir itself. Bill is sitting in a lawn chair, a few feet back from the opening in the kettle skirt. He has a long stick selected from the branch pile, and now and then pokes it into the fire, as though to remind it he is still watching.

The area around the kettle has become a kitchen of sorts. There are three lawn chairs and a couple of sitting-size tree stumps, for when we have company, and there are plastic pails standing here and there. One of these pails holds the remaining three gallons of sap from yesterday's take to be boiled off today, and all of the pails are lined with plastic sap sacks and topped with other pails tipped over to cover them, to keep the insides clean. And there are two old-fashioned metal milk cans with bail handles, also lined with plastic sacks.

We both work silently, listening to the fire, and to the sap as its song picks up volume on its way to a silent boil. I prepare the garden cart for the day's gathering. In the one-by-two-foot metal basket I keep extra liners for replacing ones that leak, and I put my gloves there when I take them off, to reduce glove loss. I have fed several pair to the sugarbush. I put the two milk cans on the cart and begin my tour.

I start as always with the three trees across the driveway. On my way back to the other trees I stop at the three between the driveway and the kettle, and then stop in the kettle kitchen and transfer the sap I've gathered into one of the plastic pails.

My cart light again, I make my way among the eleven trees east of the kettle. I am careful to not run over or step on the sapling balsam trees that have seeded from the two grand balsams next to the driveway. And I am careful, as the milk pails take on the weight of the sap, to place them over the fulcrum of the wheel axle, with the metal basket between them and the back of the cart, to hold them in place.

This part of the gathering takes about half an hour. At each tapped tree, I fold the liner down around the rim of the bucket, remove the bucket from the hook on the spile, and pour the sap into one of the collection pails. Then I return the bucket to its hook, and reposition the top flaps of the liner around the spile and under the bail. If this procedure is not done right, the motion of the pail in wind will twist the liner under the spile, and the sap will escape from the bag and out and down the trunk of the tree. I work patiently, stopping often to listen to the flicker announce its presence, an irritated, jackhammered *ta-da-da-da-dah, ta-da-da-da-dah*. And I pull the cart slowly between the trees and then back to the kettle, the sap gulping in the covered cans.

I sit then a minute with Bill and rest, and we talk about today's sap run, which we will cook the next day, and how long we think it will take to finish today's batch. And then I resume my rounds, after emptying the milk cans into the storage pails. The sap in the closest maple, the one by the dog yard, I empty directly into a holding pail, then I carry the two milk cans to the last two trees south of the house, the ones we tapped last. All of their bounty would easily fit in one can, but carrying two provides better balance. When I return to the kettle, I add this sap to the rest.

Two of the five-gallon storage pails are about three-quarters full. That means that on this second day of gathering we have acquired about eight gallons of sap, the same as yesterday. Bill has the fire well settled, the sap is at a low boil, and now, an hour or more after I joined Bill in the sugarbush, we return to the house, leaving the kettle to do its work. An hour later one of us returns to the kettle and replenishes the fire, and again an hour after that. We will do this five or six times, at some point adding the remainder of yesterday's sap, until this day's batch is reduced to about a gallon. Then we will bring it in to the kitchen stove and finish it off.

With each trip outside to tend the fire, we dip the long-handled steel ladle into the hot sap. The ladle is cold from hanging on the back of a lawn chair in the forty-degree air. The sap cools instantly, and we test it with a tongue lick, and then sip at it.

As the day progresses, so does the sap, and the taste of maple emerges and then intensifies. At first it is merely a sweetness. By midafternoon it has turned from gray-beige to light amber, is clearly maple, and begs to be drunk. By late afternoon it commands respect, an essence that bursts on the tongue. It is not syrup yet, and certainly not candy or sugar, but it is what brought us out of the house, out of winter, and into the circle of the trees.

Anininaatig: The Sacred Maple

IN THE TIME OF the *onaabanigiisis,* the Moon of the Crust on the Snow, the Ojibwe people who wintered on the shore of the big lake that would be called Superior packed their goods and journeyed to *noopiming,* "away from the big lakes," to the interior of the land that would be called the states of Minnesota and Wisconsin. They went to their sugar camps, to places that today bear city names such as Maple Grove, Maple Lake, Sugarcreek, Sugar Hill, Sugarbush.

The traditional Ojibwe people read the weather and the woods the way we read books today. They watched the animal tribes and the bird tribes and the twigs and the soil. At *ishpibiboon,* the time when the bald eagles returned in the spring, they knew it would soon be time to harvest *ziinzi-baakwadwaaboo,* sap, from *anininaatig,* the maple, the tree of *inini,* the human being.

In preparation for their spring departure, the people stored away the provisions to be left at the winter camp. Then they moved on to the women's sugarbushes, which would be passed on to their daughters, and when they arrived there, they took out the provisions stored there the previous year.

They dug the *akik,* the trade kettle, out of the ground, where it was stored, not to protect it from theft, but out of respect, to protect it from the weather, the way drums are wrapped when they are not in use.

Under *iskigamizige-giizis,* Sugarbush Moon, the women made birch bark baskets, and the men made shingles from cedar, or *negwaakwaan,* spiles from

Traditional Indian sugar camp, undated. *Courtesy Beltrami County Historical Society, Bemidji, Minnesota.*

sumac branches, which have soft centers. And then the men and the women visited each *anini-naatig*, tree of the human, and sprinkled a little tobacco on the ground at the north side of the tree and said thank you.

The men used blades to open a hole in the tree, and they placed a cedar shingle under each tap hole, or a sumac spout into the hole. And *ziinzi-baakwadwaaboo* flowed from the tree as it does yet today, and the Ojibwe people gathered the sap and carried it to the *akik*.

And while they worked and sat around the fire where the sap turned into syrup, they told stories. They told stories for fun, and stories with a purpose, and some stories that still can be told only in the presence of, the context of, the trees, the way some stories still can be told only in the presence of the drum. To recount these tales otherwise would be as to talk behind the back of another person.

When the first syrup of the season was ready, it was eaten at a ritual meal and only after that could *Nase'aawangwe*, maple sugar, be made.

Most of the syrup was made into sugar. When it was at the right stage it was poured into wooden troughs cut in logs and was stirred until it granulated. It was stirred with a *mitigwemikwaan,* a wooden spoon that sometimes had animal images carved into its handle, and was passed on within the family, or buried with its owner.

Most of the sugar was put into storage baskets. It would be used all year to season meats, the way we use salt and pepper today, and to season other foods. In the century after the European people came, sugar would be used for trading, along with furs.

From the beginning, no doubt, some sugar was made into *ziinzibaakwadoonsan,* candy. Indentations were made in the snow and filled with the ready-to-harden syrup, the origin of Sugar-on-Snow made popular by Laura Ingalls Wilder in *Little House in the Big Woods.* Some sugar was poured into small birch bark cones, and some into star- and leaf- and other shaped molds cut into flat sticks, the origin of today's maple-leaf candies.

Sugar was carried to ceremonies in miniature birch bark canoes.

Some sugar was carried from one campsite to the next, some was stored underground to be retrieved later or used on return to the sugar camp. A pit was dug and lined with moss and leaves. This was lined with birch bark, and the baskets of sugar were set in and covered with more birch bark, which was covered with more moss and leaves. Sapling strips were laid parallel across the top to keep deer from feasting there, since these animals would not walk on the thin strips for fear of breaking their slender ankles.

The Ojibwe people knew the sap run was about to end when *ziinzibaakwadwaaboo* turned a certain color, "buddy," sugarers call it today, the color of sap that comes from trees in bud. And as the Ojibwe had prepared to come to the sugar camp, they now prepared to move to their garden camp, where they would plant crops and make canoes.

From there they would go to the berry fields, then back to the garden for harvest. Then to the watery fields of the wild rice, and then back to the big lakes, to the winter camps, where they would hunt and trap, and get ready for *onaabanigiisis*, the Moon of the Crust on the Snow, when they would travel to the sugarbush, to be with *anininaatig*, the tree of *inini*, the sacred maple.

A Primer for the

Novice Sugarer

FROM TREE TO TABLE:
AN OVERVIEW

Sap from any kind of maple tree can be used to make syrup. The process is easy. Simply tap a tree, collect the sap, and boil it down. One tree usually yields one to three gallons of sap per day. One gallon of sap usually yields one-third to one-half cup of syrup. That's right, one-third to one-half cup.

Sugar maple (*Acer saccharum*) *a*, flowering branch; *b*, sterile flower; *c*, stamen; *d*, fruit with one carpel cut open to show the seed. *New Century Dictionary*, D. Appelton-Century Co., New York & London, 1927.

The ratio is approximately forty gallons of sap to one gallon of syrup.

Sap flows when the temperature gets above forty degrees Fahrenheit during the day and below freezing at night, usually during early March. The sap run can last a few days or many weeks. Whatever the length of the season, the pleasure of sugaring work will equal the pleasure of its rewards.

TAPPING THE TREES

When the weather begins to ripen, I get out the taps, also called spiles or spouts. These are essential to the sugaring process, are the road the sap travels from tree to pail. In the past, for about half of our taps, we used three-inch lengths of half-inch copper tubing, available at hardware stores and service stations. But now we have twenty aluminum spiles from a sugaring supply house (we use the Reynolds Sugar Bush catalog, Aniwa, Wisconsin, 54408). These have built-in hooks, so we don't have to cart around nails to make pail hooks, as we did for the copper tube taps.

Although I wash the spiles at the end of the sugaring season, I do it again at the beginning. I don't use soap, which may leave an untasty residue. Instead, I put the spiles in a kettle, pour boiling water over them, and let them sit. While they soak, I take out the collection pails and rinse them with hot water to remove any dust accrued since last spring's cleanup.

We're still using an electric power drill to tap our trees, with a drill-bit size to match the taps, using several heavy-duty extension cords to extend our reach into the sugarbush. Some sugarers use battery-powered drills, ones strong enough to handle frozen wood. A backup battery prevents interruption by battery rundown. A good battery can handle up to fifty trees before requiring a recharge.

All of our trees are well over the ten- to twelve-inch minimum diameter required for tapping, and many are big enough, according to some standards, to tolerate two taps, but we think that is impolite to do and never do more than one.

We choose a tap site on the tree that is free of disfigurement such as boles and is at least twelve inches away from previous tap holes. The height of the tap on the tree is inconsequential.

If a tap stays dry when others are running, we try another place on the tree. We almost always first try the side facing south, which lore declares to be more productive than the shadier surfaces, but sometimes we use the east, west, and even north surfaces, in that order.

We remember each year to aim the drill toward the center of the tree, to drill at a slight upward angle, and to go no deeper than two inches. The best sap is closest to the surface, and deeper holes are vulnerable to rot. We also remember to be careful pounding in spiles. They must be snug, and set in enough to hold the weight of the pail, but not so far as to crack the wood, which might allow sap to leak out around the tap. When we used copper taps, we placed a three-inch nail hook a few inches above the spile and pounded it in no farther than necessary to make it secure.

If we skip a year of sugaring, I go out into the grove during the summer, read the leaves, and mark the maples again. I'm always surprised that I can't remember every one, even after so many years, and that—with no help from us (plugging the holes is actually harmful)—the tap holes seal themselves so cleverly that they are difficult to find just a year or two later.

To release the sap from maples, aluminum taps, or spiles, are gently pounded into a two-inch-deep hole drilled into the tree. The sap flows out through the tap into a bucket that hangs from the hook above the tap.

PICKING THE SAP

We used to change collection systems almost every year, but at last we have settled on one that pleases us. The rejected systems include five-quart ice cream pails, which overflowed in good years, and five-gallon deli pails without liners, which got sticky and icky. And both systems left our harvest vulnerable to rain and snow contamination.

We could have bought sugaring pails, which have lids, or self-contained sap bags, which enclose the spile, but we didn't want to spend the money. In the end, our solution was so simple we were amazed it took us years to think of it.

We now buy pail liners from a sugaring supply house. These are strong plastic bags that fit nicely into our five-gallon deli pails. We put the sack in the pail, and hang the pail on the spile hook. Then we poke a hole in the plastic for the spile and push the sack over the spile and against the tree. Then we tuck the rest of the sack opening under the wire bail, so rain and snow cannot get in. Finally, we check to make sure the path for the sap droplets is clear, so they do not catch in the excess plastic folds and run out onto the ground.

The liners keep the sap clean and are easy to install and replace. I think any food-safe plastic bag would work, but the ones from the catalog are a good size, and a good strength, and are economically priced. Now when we strain the sap into the kettle, our straining cloth does not get full of bugs and leaves and, when it rains or snows, we don't have to wonder how much water we collected with the sap.

We pick every day, twice if the run is good. We load the empty collection buckets onto the garden cart and pull it from tree to tree. If a pail has a quart or more of sap in it, we pull the top of the liner down around the rim of the bucket, lift the bucket off the hook, and pour the sap from the bucket into a collection pail. After placing the bucket back on the tree and adjusting the liner, we cover the collection pail, so the sap doesn't slop out as we make our way over the rough ground.

Back at the cooking kettle, we pour the sap from the collection pails into lined storage pails. Later we will pour it from the storage pails into the cooking kettle.

We cook every day that we have at least eight gallons of sap on hand, keeping the unused sap in a storage container in a cool place. Sap starts to go sour after one or two days, unless it is good and cold (sometimes the weather takes care of that), and we always store it out of direct sun. Once when we had more sap than we could finish, I boiled a ham in it. Mmmmmm, mmmmmm. Once we made maple sap–rhubarb wine. Delectable.

Afternoon shadows in our backyard sugarbush.

COOKING THE SAP

Approximately 98 percent of maple sap is water. Remove most of the water by evaporation, and you have maple syrup. Remove a little more water, and you have maple sugar or candy.

Maple sap is reduced to maple syrup by boiling off the water. This boiling process is best accomplished outdoors, where the steam, which contains some sugar, will not coat walls and cupboards, or soak up into wallpaper. Remember that sixteen cups of sap (one gallon) reduced to one-half to one-third cup of syrup will release into the air approximately fifteen and one-half cups of water.

Wood, coal, gas, and electricity are good heat sources for boiling down sap. A kettle or pan with a large surface area should be used to hold the sap.

The first time we sugared we wanted to start out small, so we took two deep, electric frying pans outside, plugged them in, and simmered sap in them. It took a long time, but worked, and we got a half-pint of syrup. Encouraged, we thought about using a stock pot or canning kettle over a fire, but finally cleaned up the huge cast-iron trade kettle, which we'd bought for the scorching step of finishing wild rice, a project we abandoned in abject frustration.

Over the years we developed an evaporating system that worked. In the trade kettle, over a wood fire, we start with about five gallons of sap. That is a minimum amount for our large trade kettle, but if we were cooking in a smaller pot, we could start with one or two gallons.

We bring the sap to a brisk boil, so the water will evaporate into steam and blow away. As the total amount in the kettle reduces, we add more sap, a gallon or two at a time, to keep it at the original level until the day's take is used up, or until we're too tired to stay out any longer.

In six to ten hours, we can reduce ten to twenty gallons of sap to about one gallon of near-syrup. As it cooks, it darkens, but does not thicken discernibly. We keep a long-handled metal soup ladle handy, for checking the progress of the color from

Forty gallons of maple sap boils down to one gallon of maple syrup. We harvest about twenty gallons of sap a day, which takes about six hours to boil off in this cast-iron kettle, and another two hours to finish off on the kitchen stove. We average four pint jars of syrup (one-half gallon) for each day the sap flows. In an average year, we can get about four to five gallons of syrup. *Photos by Vivienne Morgan.*

clear to dark amber, and for occasionally stirring the sap, although that is not necessary.

When we are almost down to that desired one gallon, we gradually take fire away from the kettle so the precious few quarts of near-syrup won't scorch. Always, at any time, we are prepared to stop a boil-up. If there is still snow on the ground, we can grab a handful and toss it in. If the snow is gone, we keep a quart of sap handy and use that. When there is so little sap left in the kettle, if a boil-up is not caught right away, we're left with a candy-coated kettle and no syrup.

Using a shallow two-cup stainless steel bowl, and then a large soup ladle, we dip and pour the dark, hot sap into a five-quart kitchen kettle, filtering it as we pour through several layers of felt filters set in a colander on top of the pot. If we waited until we got into the house to do the filtering, the sap would cool enough so that it would just sit in the filter.

In the house, over the kitchen stove, this one gallon of near-syrup, originally ten to twenty gallons of sap, will yield about two to four pints of finished syrup.

FINISHING OFF

During the summer, I buy every pint and half-pint canning jar I find at garage sales. Maple syrup is for giving, and the jars don't come back. About the time we put in our test taps, I load the dishwasher with spidery, dusty jars and gave them their first washing.

When I bring the near-syrup into the house for finishing, I heat up a kettle of water and pour it over a few jars and their lids and rings, along with tongs for handling and a funnel for filling the jars. I do this while closely watching the sap. I avoid the temptation to stir it, as that folds cool air into the kettle and increases cooking time. In an hour or so, a gallon of near-syrup derived from twenty gallons of sap will reduce down to about two pints of finished syrup.

The syrup is ready to be canned when it consistently draws two beads at the same time from a metal spoon. (This is about 248 degrees on a candy thermometer, but we prefer the spoon test because the near-syrup is now shallow enough in the pan that a thermometer is not always accurate.) When the liquid drizzles from the spoon in one line, it is not close to being done. When two beads start to form but drip alternately, it *is* close. If it gets to the stage of sheeting or aproning on the spoon, it has cooked too much. It will look fine when you first can it, but later it is likely to crystallize in the jars, forming rock candy. It looks pretty, but it clings to the glass, and you can't get it out. Each crystal is a drop of maple syrup lost forever.

I keep the syrup hot while filling the jars by setting the pot back on the burner between fillings. After tightening the lids, I turn the jars sideways so the hot syrup resterilizes the lids.

We store our sealed jars on the shelf on the basement stairway. Opened jars and ones that didn't seal tight we keep in the fridge, or heat to a near-bubble in the microwave and seal again. Some people store syrup in the freezer, where it keeps forever.

When the sap quits running, or when it turns milky, we use a hammer to pull the taps from the trees. We leave the holes open. They will seal at their own pace. Then we wash all of the equipment—spiles, pails, everything—in lots of very hot water, without soap. Soap residue is almost impossible to get off, and can taint the syrup. Finally, we put everything in clean plastic bags to be stored away for the summer, fall, and winter that must pass before the next sugar harvest.

SUGARING WITH PIPELINES

We were curious about the pipelines now being used by many commercial and some home sugarers, so I looked into them. While pails have to be emptied, and their contents transported to the sugarhouse, a plastic tubing setup allows the sap to flow from the tree to a collection point, or even to the sugarhouse itself.

To my surprise, few Minnesota sugarers use pipelines. Though we are said to have the sweetest trees in the country, our season is not as long as New England's, and most sugarers, even those who sell their product, are satisfied with collecting sap by hand.

But sugarers who tap thousands of trees find it well worth both the effort and the cost to invest in a pipeline. Special taps are used to accommodate the plastic tubing. The tubes from the trees are connected to longer runs of tubes that link many trees together. Some operations use gravity to get the sap to the tanks or sugarhouse, and some use vacuum pumps, which can increase sap output.

As with conventional taps, the pipelines have to be tended. They must be watched for leaks and for damage from animals. They have to be flushed clean at the end of the season, and the chloride-based cleaning solvent has to be rinsed out as well. Squirrels like sap, and they are happy to chew through a little plastic to get to it.

Information on pipeline systems is usually available from departments of agriculture and natural resources in states where maple sap is harvested.

Section 11

Hiatus

IN NORTHERN MINNESOTA IN late March or early April *Haliaeetus leucocephalus,* the bald eagle, returns from its winter sojourn. The ice is still on the lakes but the eagle does not care. It dines on mice and squirrels, and on the carcasses of deer that have fallen to the winter.

From the west window of our house I can see an animal that died on the bay of our lake. Or rather, I can see the flock of crows that rises and settles there all day long, and the half-dozen bald eagles that come and go when they please, and the three dogs that come from nowhere at dusk, hunker down, and work at the remains.

This has gone on for three days now. At first I watched with binoculars through the window, then I got out the telescope and went outside. Still I could not identify the humps of hide. Whatever the beast, maybe a deer, I don't know how it died, or why it died here within my sight, or even when. It could have happened months ago and only now emerged from the melting snow.

On each of these three days, I divide my attention between the feast of scavengers on the ice to the west of the house and the sugarbush to the east. The weather is cold again, and the sap is not really flowing. Each noon, on my way to or from the mailbox, I make rounds of the sap pails and mentally tote up the take. Even though it has stayed below forty, some of the taps run a little. A few quarts total. Then a gallon or two. Finally, today, several gallons.

I bring the mail in and alert Bill. Tomorrow we can sugar again. Many of the taps are damp and by tomorrow there should be enough for the kettle.

Crows, not eagles, are really the first birds to return after winter, but they are unreliable. They come back even during the winter, then they leave. Then they return, and leave again. They are more a reflection of the weather than harbingers of spring.

I think of them this week as I fuss about the ebb and flow of the sugar tide. If I really turned myself over to the season as I claim to do, I would not be irritated by the lapses in the sap flow. Rather, I would enjoy the breaks, even be grateful for them. Instead I fret. What if this is the end of it? What if it gets warm now and stays warm? What if it gets warm and the trees start to bud, and then it gets cold again, but the sap has gone buddy?

It is not winter. It is not spring. It is the cusp between seasons. The pussy willows in the ditch by the road are out, little mottled gray thumbs on magenta stems. The snowfall from the first day of the cold snap is not yet melted. The eagles are back and will not leave until after the lakes freeze in the fall.

The sap is waiting to renew its journey in the maple trees. In the house I wash jars for syrup, reread my sugaring journal, watch weather reports and our own thermometer. Bill and I play chess. And I watch the crows and the eagles on the glaring white snow on the bay.

The Circle of the Trees

APRIL FIRST. APRIL FOOL'S DAY. It is more than three weeks since we set the test taps in four maples, and we now have three batches of syrup: eight pints, or one gallon, from forty gallons of sap. Ten gallons of raw sap wait in holding pails out by the *akik*. Around noon, Bill goes out and starts the fire, and a little later I go out and pick sap. Yesterday the spiles were almost running rather than dripping. This morning it was already forty degrees when I got up at seven, and I wonder if the sap ran all night and will keep running today as the temperature rises, or if the pressure is off and the trees will keep their treasure to themselves.

Yesterday it got up to fifty degrees. We worked outside in sweatshirts, gloveless and hatless. We could actually hear the snow melting around us. It warms from the ground as well as from the sun, and the old snow beneath the newer top crust gives in first and creates chambers under the heaps of snow. The upward melting weakens the infrastructure, which finally gives way, and since I was close by, and there was no wind, and because I was listening, when the under-ceiling of the snow fell I could hear the crystals crash in upon each other.

It is quiet today as well. Crows call. Robins continue their eternal effort at a meaningful tune. Bluebirds come and go from the bluebird house, checking out the facilities. The sky is clear except for thin skiffs of white clouds, and the dissipating chalk line of one jet contrail.

I walk slowly between the trees, pulling my cart, the pails jangling pleasantly against each other. In most of the grove there are only smatterings of snow, and even the puddled remains of larger drifts are mostly sunk into the earth. Where there is some kind of shade, a fallen branch, a handful of leaves, there is also ice. I walk carefully, reading with my feet the lumpy Braille of the ground.

Otherwise I do not think while I work. I move among the trees the way the animals do, purposeful and without guile. It is different from merely walking in the woods, and different from a morning walk on our country road, where the smell of the air and the subtle sounds of place feed thought.

Here in the sugarbush I am not a philosopher, not a voyeur, not a wanderer. In some ways I am not even human. I am one of the animals that wakes when the eagle returns and joins the trees in preparation for the next season. My impatience melted with the snow, and I am no longer in a hurry. I graze from tree to tree, feeding on the odor of leaves in mulch, on the conversation of birds, on the randy play of squirrels.

I am without hope. I am without dismay. I am without prayer. I am without awe. I have no mercy. No compassion. There is no anger in my heart. As the trees take water from the earth, I take water from the trees. It sustains me, and I am comforted.

I begin to understand the hunter, the man and the woman who enter the forest with intent to kill although they are not aggrieved by their prey and do not want for food.

They do not seek to be out in nature, to admire from a path the conversion of plants to dust, or to wonder at the girth of a tree that has seen more history than any human ever will.

They seek to be of nature. To lay down the burden of the clock, of desire, of the need for redemption. They do not enter the woods with a craving to kill, but with the hope of gathering food for the table, and sitting again with the family they miss, their cousins the trees, their uncles the deer, their aunts the birds.

Perhaps. Perhaps that is why a human with no need for killed flesh goes into the forest and kills.

It is why I draw water from the well of *anini-naatig,* the tree of *inini,* the maple.

Forty Acres

IN 1914 THE LOG CABIN on the hill overlooking the southeast bay of Mud Lake basked in the shade of six acres of hardwood balsam, spruce, elm, maple, basswood, willow, and oak. The trees were part of the north woods, a dark and seemingly eternal forest that bridged the geological gap between the farther north conifer woods and the farther south broadleaf woods.

Eighty years later, in 1994 the log cabin is the living room of our house. Each family that has lived here, including Bill and myself, has added on to the cabin: kitchen, bath, bedroom, bedroom, studio, utility room, garage, porch.

The forty acres of the homestead and the six acres surrounding the house have also changed. In the

1940s there was a barn, but it is gone now, as is the wind-catching lilac hedge that ran south to north along the top of the hill that falls down to the swamp.

In the 1940s, the swamp was floating bog, firm enough to drive a horse on. There was even a road of sorts, with a ford in the creek that separates this side of the swamp from the other side. Today the peat moss mat is half afloat, half anchored to ground, nailed down by willow saplings. Dark channels of water still underpin all of the growth, and walking on the bog now is treacherous, the integrity of the mat broken by the progress of land.

The land that surrounds the bog has also evolved, though not always through its own natural processes. Once mixed forest of hardwood and conifer, it was logged relentlessly in the early 1900s, and the timber of the north woods was sent south and east and even west to build the new cities of America. As with much of the land in the upper Midwest, the once-shaded acreage surrounding Mud Lake and its swamps was left open to the stare of the sun.

The maple and similar species of the early forests did not seed well in bright light, and the seedlings that were not trampled by the loggers and their horses and wagons and sleds curled into themselves and died. But aspen and birch saplings like the sun, and happily filled the air with their lithe stems and light green leaves.

Not every inch of the northern forests was shipped away as lumber. Loggers had families, and homes, and homesteads, and they knew the comfort of trees. As with many log cabin sites, the six acres surrounding the house on the southeast corner of Mud Lake was not logged. The oak and maple on the hillside were left uncut, as were the maple and elm and oak and basswood and willow that surround the house.

Most of the trees in the grove east of the house are maples, the ones we keep company with each March and April. The elms are gone, given over to disease. The oaks seem to prefer the far side of the garage, and the willows hang out in the low spot on the far side of the driveway.

We are not the only ones grateful for the old maples. Squirrels live in them, gray and red. Songbirds like the winged seeds that helicopter to the ground. And now, as this generation reaches its dotage, woodpeckers, downy, hairy, pileated, join our habitat family and mark for us the trees that are ailing.

Many of our trees seem to be dying. Branches are broken, and moss climbs more than the north sides of the trunks. We are cautious tapping, no more than one spile to a tree, though the girth of most could justify two or even three, and we skipped sugaring three years in a row when we had drought.

It is sad to watch the passing of a forest, even one in miniature. It reminds us that we too are moving along the perimeter of the circle of our life, and will one day come to the place where we entered, which is also the place we exit. And when we are gone, what we did is no longer circumscribed by our presence, and flies loose into the world.

So it is with the trees. When these old maples tumble, the light will pour through the holes they leave, and something new will grow there. In our grove, it will likely be more maple, and some balsam, because the community of seniors provides the quiet shade preferred for their germination. We watch for saplings as we tread the grove. They grow slowly now, settling in, and they will grow slowly until chance gives them their own piece of the sky. Then they will scramble to keep their place, and will one day shelter seedlings.

Even the old hardwood neighborhoods now inhabited by aspen and birch will likely be resettled by the maple and its friends. Aspen and birch saplings will not grow in the shadow of their parents. The parents instead will nurse the patient seeds such as those of the maple that wait in the soil for calm, cool shade. They will germinate, and take root, and when the aspen and birch expire, the maple and its kind will climb into the sun.

Sugar Camp

ROLLAND GREW UP IN the log cabin that is our living room. In the 1920s and '30s, a "tote road," a wagon trail between towns, cut across the south field and along the east edge of the homestead's forty acres. Between the tote road and the house stood the grove of trees that is now our sugarbush.

Rolland and his father did not sugar there. Twenty trees were not worth the effort. Instead they hitched up the horses to the sleigh and went to their sugar camp: west from the house, down the hill to the meadow that is now a swamp, across the meadow and the ford in the creek, up the slope on the other side, past grandma's house, and out onto the peninsula that separates our bay of Mud Lake from the lake itself.

© Terri Anderson, Leonard, Minnesota.

The road down the peninsula was wide enough for the sleigh, but there was also room in the woods to drive the team among the trees themselves. The shrubby undergrowth that keeps humans at arm's length today requires warmth and good sun. The old forests were cool and dark, in summer the crowns of the mature trees holding hands to keep the sun at bay.

In March, in the daylight, Rolland and his father took the sleigh and team and went to the sugarbush on the point. Using a breast drill, they tapped the trunks of two hundred maples. Into each hole they tapped a spile, a curl of metal, fashioned at home. On each spile they hung a metal pail with a little tin roof to keep out snow, rain, leaves, and the dust of the forest.

Every morning and evening, Rolland and his dad made the rounds of the sugarbush to pick sap, guiding the team and sleigh along the snow path between the trees. They emptied the collection pails into five-gallon milk cans and took the whole lot back to the "arch," the place where they boiled off. At the end of the morning pick, Rolland returned home to sleep. At the end of the evening pick, Rolland's father returned home.

Breast drill.

Rolland stayed at the sugar camp all night, boiling one to two hundred gallons of sap, as his father had done during the day. One at a time, as the level lowered, he lifted the five-gallon cans and added sap to the metal evaporating pan, four feet by two feet by ten inches deep, that they'd had made in town. He teased at the fire to keep it hot but not too hot, and sometimes he lay back on the ground and listened to the conversation of the nighttime forest.

When the day's sap run was boiled down to about half an inch in the pan, Rolland poured it off, back into the five-gallon milk cans. In the morning, his father came with the team and the sleigh, and they made the rounds of the taps, and took the sap to the arch, and Rolland took the cans with the near-syrup and went across the creek, and across the meadow, and up the hill to the log cabin.

His mother finished the syrup at the kitchen stove. She poured it into kitchen pans and kept the fire hot but not too hot; and when the syrup drew two beads from a metal spoon, she poured it off into jugs and corked it. When they went to town, they took along a few jugs of maple syrup to trade and to sell.

When Rolland married he no longer sugared on the point, but he and Jenny helped sugar at a neighbor's. For as far as one could walk in the forest, it seemed, pails hung from trees. Families gathered. The grownups hung out around the fire, talking. The children ran into the trees and back, never getting too far away. The young adults volunteered to pick at the farthest trees, the ones out of sight where, the stories say, there was kissing. At the end of the day, the near-syrup was taken into the house and the women finished it at the stove.

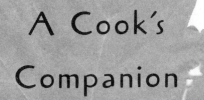

A Cook's
Companion

USING MAPLE SYRUP

Maple syrup is best employed in its pure state on pancakes/waffles/French toast, hot cereal, squash, and yams or sweet potatoes. Some aficionados claim that it surpasses chocolate as a topping for vanilla ice cream. It glazes pork and ham. It is good in tea and coffee. It is decadent when drizzled on hot, fresh popcorn (microwave popcorn works best) and is enjoyed twice because it must be licked off of fingers.

Maple syrup's delicate flavor is most powerful when it makes direct contact with the tongue. That flavor tends to disappear when the syrup is used as one of many ingredients in cake or other cooked goods and dishes. Still, in most recipes, maple syrup can be substituted in equal amounts for molasses, honey, corn syrup, white sugar, and brown sugar. When substituting maple syrup, which is liquid, for granulated sugars, decrease other liquids in the recipe, such as milk or water, by about two tablespoons for each cup of syrup used. When substituting equal amounts of maple syrup for liquid sugars, such as corn syrup, no adjustment is necessary.

Sealed jars of maple syrup may be stored in the cupboard. Once opened, they should be stored in the refrigerator. Maple syrup may also be frozen.

MAPLE SYRUP RECIPES

Because maple syrup flavor is usually lost when used in combination with other ingredients, I do not often squander my precious syrup for baking or cooking. Here are two recipes that I do recommend.

Martha's Maple Syrup Pie

1 tablespoon flour
1 tablespoon granulated white or brown sugar
1 tablespoon whole milk or half-and-half
⅔ cup whole milk or half-and-half

2 eggs, lightly beaten
1⅓ cups 100-percent maple syrup

9-inch uncooked pie shell

Mix together the flour, sugar, and 1 tablespoon milk. Add ⅔ cup milk, eggs, and maple syrup. Stir until well blended. Pour into a 9-inch pie shell. Bake at 450 degrees for 10 minutes, then 300 degrees for 35 to 40 minutes. The pie is done when the edges are set but the center still jiggles a little.

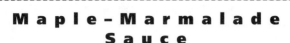

Maple–Marmalade Sauce

A perfect topping for squash, sweet potatoes, or yams.

½ cup 100-percent
  maple syrup
½ cup brown sugar

¼ cup butter, melted
¼ cup orange marmalade
¼ teaspoon ground nutmeg

Mix ingredients together thoroughly. Serve at room temperature. Store in refrigerator.

MAKING MAPLE CANDY

Microwave Maple Dollops

Soft candy, ready to eat in twenty minutes. Invite friends and children to help—everyone can take turns stirring.

Ingredient: 1 cup of 100-percent maple syrup
Yield: 12 to 18 candies

Note: To increase yield when cooking with the microwave, do not double the ingredients. Cook two batches instead.

Using the high-power setting on the microwave oven, for about 4 to 7 minutes, bring the syrup to a boil in a two-quart glass container. Continue to boil until it forms soft threads when ¼ teaspoon syrup is tested in cold water. (For comparison, test some after 2 minutes. It will disperse in the water.)

Remove the container from the microwave and stir with a metal spoon about 3 to 5 minutes until the syrup gets creamy and begins to hold its shape. Quickly drop in dollops onto waxed paper, or into butter or candy molds. It will set in a few minutes. Eat immediately, or store in refrigerator or freezer.

Microwave Maple Wax

This clear, taffylike candy is tricky to make and a challenge to eat, but worth the effort in both cases, and a not-quite-right batch is still a tasty treat.

Ingredient: 1 cup of 100-percent maple syrup
Yield: 12 to 18 candies

Note: To increase yield when cooking with a microwave, do not double ingredients. Cook two batches instead.

*Using the high-power setting on the microwave oven, for about 7 to 10 minutes, bring the syrup to a boil in a one-quart glass container. Continue to boil until it solidifies when ¼ teaspoon syrup is tested in cold water and remains brittle when removed from the water ("hard crack" stage). **Do not stir.** Immediately pour into medium-size buttered pan, such as a 9-inch square or 7-inch round cake pan.*

Allow to cool thoroughly (alas, it takes hours). It will get very hard and will shatter into pieces when cracked with the handle of a heavy knife.

Stovetop Instructions

Maple Dollops and Maple Wax can also be made on the stovetop. Double or triple the amount of the ingredients used in the microwave recipes (or the syrup will cook too fast and will burn), and use a heavy one-quart saucepan. Bring to a low simmer over medium heat, then follow directions in the recipes. The process will take two to three times longer on the stovetop than in the microwave, not because of the increase in the quantity of syrup but because a lower heat must be used to avoid burning.

COOKING WITH RAW
MAPLE SAP

Raw maple sap can be used as water for cooking vegetables, meat, and poultry. Just substitute the sap for water. The sap will impart a slightly sweet maple taste to the food cooked in it.

Maple sap can also be used to make homemade wine and beer. Again, just substitute the sap for water.

Section III

Promise

As I STAND AT the kitchen sink wetting the filters I use to strain the sap, I look down the field and to the right where a small rise in the land creates a north slope. Yes, there is still snow there. The end of it. Even the cat ice is gone now from the wet spots in the sugarbush. This afternoon when I picked sap, the leaves, the last of their moisture given off to the spring sun, crackled underfoot and under the wheels of my cart.

I squeeze the excess water out of the four sheets of felt, layer them in the colander, and set the colander in the heavy aluminum pot that was my mother's pressure cooker. The lid long ago went its own way, but this pot is perfect for finishing syrup.

It is heavy, so the syrup will not burn easily, and the sides are high, so it cannot easily boil over, though it can and does.

I retrieve the small, shallow aluminum bowl and the shallow dipper from the dishwasher, pick up one leather glove from the stand by the door, and take my apparatus out to the kettle. Bill has pulled the skirt away and is spreading out the last of the fire. In the bottom of the kettle bubbles break on the less than a gallon of near-syrup that remains from the ten gallons simmered for six hours.

I sit in one of the lawn chairs with the pot and colander on my lap and watch as Bill dips the long-handled ladle into the sap and pours it back into the kettle. It is dark amber in color, partly because it is laced with nitre, also called "sugar sand," a natural sediment in maple syrup, partly because it is getting late in the season, and partly because we boil in a trade kettle and each batch leaves behind a candied film that cooks into subsequent batches.

One holding pail of today's pick is set between me and the fire in case the sap in the kettle decides to foam up and turn to hard candy. A few table-spoons will settle it back down. The rest of the day's pick is in holding pails sitting in and beside the cart. We'll cook it tomorrow.

Around me the day quiets and prepares to shut down. The chickadees and flickers have quit their banter. The breeze has slowed, leaving silent last year's tall, dried goldenrod that fills up the empty spaces in the grove. Halfway between due west and due north, the sun closes in on the horizon.

The embers that Bill dispersed from under the kettle have given up their glow, and the coming on of the evening air has relieved the kettle of some of its heat. I move to Bill's side and hold the house pot while he reaches down with the aluminum bowl, dips out sap, and pours it into the colander. The hot bubbles settle out as the sap meets the cool, wet felt, and slowly the syrup-to-be seeps through into the pot, leaving sugar sand and kettle debris in the filters.

When only spoonfuls are left in the kettle, Bill switches to the dipper and rescues every bit that he can; then he picks up the nearby sap pail and pours a few gallons into the kettle to keep the leftovers from burning.

Balancing the pot on the rim of the kettle, I retrieve the leather glove from my pocket and use it as a hot pad so I can hold the now heavy pot in both hands, one on the perpendicular handle, one underneath, with the glove to protect my skin from the heat. Bill takes a last poke at the ashes, and we turn together and walk to the house.

Inside the door, I set the pot on a counter, take off my jacket, and hang it on the rack next to the parka I wore the first few weeks of sugaring. The aura of smoke and sugar surrounds both garments, and in few minutes, when I get the sap cooking, the perfume of maple will permeate the house.

In the kitchen, I set the pot by the sink and hold the colander up so the sap can finish draining. Then I put the colander in the sink and move the pot to the stove.

Now begins the last two hours of the day's work. Unlike the outside tasks, which can be done at leisure, this cooking takes attention and precision. I hook a candy thermometer onto the pot, turn the burner on to medium heat, and watch as bubbles seek the surface and break into air.

In a few minutes the sap is back up to a simmer, about two hundred and twenty degrees. I turn the burner down a bit, and begin the syrup–dinner dance. Get something out of the fridge, check the syrup. Start the peas cooking, check the syrup. Cross the room to set the table. Listen to the syrup.

Even in the house finishing pot, syrup sings when it is about to boil up. A slight hiss. A warning. A promise. If I hear it, and I am quick enough, I can get to the pot before it goes over, before the huge golden bubbles leap the pan and spread themselves over the stovetop and down into the burner.

If I am not quick enough, I have a mess to clean up and syrup to rescue. I take the pot to the sink, wipe off the sides and bottom, return it to a clean burner, and turn the heat on low. When the first burner is cool, I remove it and then remove the cup I'd set under it to catch overflow. Then I take a spatula and scrape up every grain of syrup that has solidified on the stovetop and put it in a bowl. We'll munch on it. I scrape the spatula clean, then lick it cleaner. If no one is looking, I lean down to the stove and lick up the last tracings with my tongue.

It happens at least once a season. Sometimes early, when I am not yet attuned to the rhythms of sugaring. Sometimes later, when I am made careless by luck. Today, as the sugar content increases in the sap in the pot, so do I reduce the heat of the burner.

When dinner is ready, I turn the burner way down so I can eat, but even then get up occasionally to inspect the dark, glossy surface. After dinner, I turn up the heat again, and also heat a teakettle full of water. While it comes to a boil I set four pint jars and a half-pint jar in the sink. Then I put five canning lids and rings, a funnel, and a pair of tongs into a bowl in the sink. When the water is ready, I pour it into the jars and the bowl, and I am ready for the syrup.

When I first brought the sap into the house it was still thin relative to syrup. It easily slipped off a metal spoon and back into the pot. As it reduced, it began to hold on the spoon but still flowed off in a single stream. Now, as it gets closer to syrup, it hangs onto the spoon and struggles to pull together into a single bead that reluctantly drops off into the pot. Soon it will not be able to manage that, will separate, and simultaneously draw two long threads on its way back to the pan.

By that time I have taken out the candy thermometer, because the level in the one-gallon pot has gone down from a few inches from the top to a few inches from the bottom, and the thermometer is no longer accurate. But the spoon is still reliable, and when the sap consistently draws two beads, I transfer the jars and lids to a clean cloth on the counter next to the stove and finish today's maple syrup.

I lift the pot by its outstretched handle and, using the funnel, fill three of the pints to a half-inch from the top. Then depending on how much is left, I fill another pint or the half-pint. Moving quickly, I set a lid on each one, then take a wet cloth in each hand

and screw the lids down, and then give them one more turn twice, and once again to be sure, and then tip them for a moment on their sides to further sterilize the lids; then I set them in a row on the counter, and I stand back and contemplate.

Three and one-half pints. A decent day's take from twenty maples. It is seven in the evening. Bill started the outside fire at eleven in the morning. I step into the living room and announce the outcome to Bill, and we talk about the ten gallons of sap sitting outside in the dusk, waiting for tomorrow's boiling, and we wonder if it will freeze tonight, and the sap will run again tomorrow, or if it will stay as warm as it is now, forty-five degrees.

And I sit for a minute before I return to wash up the sugaring dishes and rinse out the filters. The sun is at my favorite sunset trajectory. It casts a beam through the entryway window onto the side of the mahogany piano, onto the small table stacked with books, across the top of the television, casting on the far wall shadows of the trinkets we keep there, a brass elephant, a marble donkey, a glass goat, and lands last on the bookcase in the corner where it ignites a row of pictures of children, parents, siblings, and friends.

Twice each year this blade of light cuts through the armor of the house, forecasting spring or fall. It saddens me as much as it brings pleasure. Even in the timeless time of sugaring, time is passing.

Ping. A syrup jar in the kitchen seals itself, the metal lid announcing that it has yielded to the heat of the syrup and is sucked down tight against the glass rim.

Ping. The wedge of light recedes with the sun into the horizon. And later another *ping,* and then much later, the kitchen clean and settled into dark, as Bill and I are sitting in the living room, the final *ping.* It comes to me through the conversation of the television the way the clock at my grandmother's came to me through my dreams, striking the hour even in the darkest of the night.

Visitors in
the Sugarbush

I LINE UP THE maple syrup jars in columns according to the batch number written in marker on the top of each lid, along with the year. The contents of the first ones are amber, the later ones dark amber, and the most recent are the color of translucent molasses. For the commercial sugarer these last jars would be unacceptable, but they are welcome in our pantry. They come from late sap that is starting to get buddy, and from a trade kettle that harbors remnants of every batch of syrup cooked.

A thin layer of dark dust floats at the bottom of each jar. Sugar sand. Malate of lime. Nitre.

Commercial operations filter out all of it, and we get rid of some, but always there is some left. It begins to settle out right away and in a year will be like a firm wafer clinging to the bottom of the jar. It is harmless. A bit crunchy. Bill likes to eat it.

I pick one of the darkest jars out of the lot, unscrew the ring, and pop the lid off with a can opener. We have company today, sugaring company, and we are going to make candy. I pour the half-pint of syrup into a two-quart glass measuring cup, stopping when I get to the sugar sand. Then I put the cup in the microwave and set it for three minutes.

This is our fourth batch of visitors. Some people, when we tell them we sugar, are not interested beyond a few polite questions. But some others respond with their eyes as well as their comments. "Sugaring? Making maple syrup? You do that? Can I come see?"

"Yes, come see. And help, too." And when the sap is running, I make phone calls to friends and we make promises to each other.

I remember driving by sugarbushes before we moved to Mud Lake. I liked looking at the patient pails hanging on the trees, and wondered what it was like to farm maples. Now when friends coast into the driveway we can see them pointing to the buckets and they ooh and ahh as they get out of the car, and we saunter over to them, and they to us, and we sugar.

We start at the nearest tree, to admire the tick, tick of the sap droplets, and each of us catches a few in our palms, licks them up with our tongues, and tastes, and

Sonya and Danny Clemenson catch a few drops of maple sap, which is clear and tastes like slightly sweet water. *Photo by William H. McDowall.*

considers. Some can sense maple, some not. But we all go back for seconds. Water pumped by a tree from the well of the earth carries more sweet than sugar accounts for.

Then we move on to the kettle, city dwellers at first tripping over the lumpy ground with its hidden branches and matted clumps of leaves, and Bill stirs the fire, and we all lean over the kettle and listen to the sap and comment on its color. "Like cinnamon and sugar," says a child.

And Bill fills the long-handled dipper and passes it around, and everyone takes a sip of the sap-to-be-syrup, and heads nod and someone says "yes, that's maple," and we stand around the *akik,* moving out of the smoke that seems to follow us, and those who are curious about wood inspect our supply, and those who know fire discuss draft, and some sit in the lawn chairs and watch the chickadees in the trees and the clouds in the sky.

Then we put them to work. I show them how to unhook and rehook the sack liners in the baskets,

Visitors to our sugarbush, Rose and Will Weaver, pick sap.

and how to pour the sap into the collecting pails, and I point out the trees to the north and east and west, and Bill and I stand by the kettle and watch Will and Rose, Hilda, Mary and Andy and Sonya and Danny, Vivienne and Michael make their way through the grove, talking to each other, fussing at the taps, and proudly returning with their take.

It is like watching a movie of ourselves. I pick sap in three sets, resting in between and telling Bill about the trees, which one is slow, which is hot, which is not behaving like itself. And then we stand around the kettle and Bill dips some sap and we sip at it and cluck about its goodness.

When the sap is picked and settled in the holding pails, and the pictures are taken, and Bill has the fire set for an hour or so, we go into the house and drink something cold and make candy.

I used to make it on the stove. It took an hour or two, and I sometimes sacrificed a whole quart to the miracle of crystallization. I never did get the pretty little maple-leaf candies that I wanted. There's about a five-second leeway between pourable sugar and sugar concrete, which is maple sugar in its most serious form. I've had to pry it out of the pot with a screwdriver and pound it into granules with a mallet.

Then I discovered microwave candy. One cup to a batch, a few minutes to cook, and the company does the stirring.

Today, every thirty seconds I take the boiling-up syrup out of the microwave and test a drop in cold water. The first time, it disperses like thin oil. The next, it drifts to the bottom of the cup. Finally it congeals when I push it with the spoon, then it forms soft treads, and is ready.

I hand the measuring cup with a metal spoon in it to the nearest person at the table and say, "Stir." And she stirs, and passes it to him, and he stirs, and he passes it back. And after a few minutes the clear, dark syrup is the color of butterscotch and is staying in streaks on the side of the cup, and then it holds its shape when the spoon moves through it, and I say, "Quick!" and take the cup and scoop teaspoonfuls into rubber maple-leaf molds. And by the time I have done a dozen candies the first ones are nearly set and the syrup left in the bowl is hard.

The guests stare, and I break off the drippings between the leaves and pass them around, and we all sit in silence with crumbs of essence of maple bursting on our tongues. I get a table knife and scrape the inside of the measuring cup, pushing the maple dust out onto waxed paper, and we all wet a finger and dip and lick.

And then the candies are set and I turn them out, and first one of us and then another reaches over and moves them into a row, or turns them this way or that.

Early in this season, Bill's ten-year-old grandson came to help. He drilled the last two trees we tapped, including the biggest one in the grove, and he told Bill "the sap just squirted out," and we call it Chabin's tree. He helped with the fire and the wood, and the picking of sap, and he helped make candy.

He thought it would be just candy, or just syrup that was solid, but it rendered him silent. He licked spoons. He scraped drippings off the stove. I put scraps in a custard cup and he carried it around the house, dipping into it with a wet finger until the cup was empty.

We packed a little box of maple leaves for him to take home, as we do for all of our conspirators, along with a pint of syrup. The phone call comes the next morning: "We had pancakes for dinner last night, with maple syrup. We could come out again, if you need more help."

Grandpa McDowall and grandson Chabin Blanc set a maple tap and hang a pail to catch the sap.

Sugar Shack

CARMEN AND ROBERT AND their son Douglas and I are standing in the kitchen of their house in rural central Minnesota, one hundred and fifty miles south of Mud Lake. "It gets in your blood," says Carmen. It is the only explanation she has for twenty-six years of sugaring history.

They started the year Douglas was born. They tapped trees on their land and cooked it off in a metal washtub. The next year they had evaporating pans made and built a small sugar shack. After six or seven years, they built a bigger sugar shack and bought equipment.

We exit the house through the garage and walk up a little slope to a concrete-block building. The house and outbuildings are surrounded by woods, and in every direction I see commercial sap sacks hanging on trees. We go in the door of the sugar house, and right through and out the back door.

"Might as well start at the beginning," says Robert, and he points to the two-hundred gallon collecting tank on wheels that is hooked up to a small tractor. Each day he and Carmen and Douglas and Douglas's wife make the rounds of the sacks, pour them into the tank, and bring it back to the shack. Between us and the tractor is a four-hundred gallon tank, on stilts. The sap is pumped up into this tank, which has a pipe running into the sugar-house.

We return inside and with his finger Robert traces the flow of the sap through the system. The pipe coming through the concrete wall leads to an enclosed steel evaporator, two by six by six feet, that fills the space between floor and ceiling. It is completely contained, but has little doors here and there for peering inside. The lower two feet is the heating unit, the middle two feet the boiling unit, the top is the exhaust system.

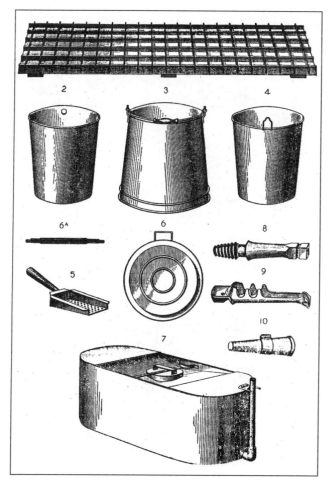

Sugar-making utensils: 1, sugar mold; 2 and 4, sap buckets; 3, gathering pail; 5, skimmer; 6, cover for sap bucket; 6a, cross-section of same; 7, gathering tank; 8, 9, and 10, sap spouts. *U.S. Department of Agriculture, Farmers' Bulletin, Number 252, 1906.*

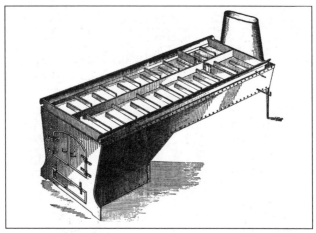

Maple-sap evaporator. *U.S. Department of Agriculture, Farmers' Bulletin, Number 252, 1906.*

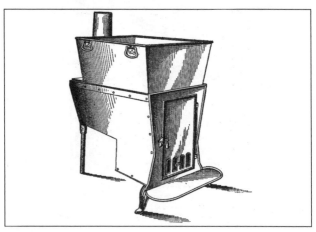

Sugaring-off arch. *U.S. Department of Agriculture, Farmers' Bulletin, Number 252, 1906.*

I stick my face into one of the openings to the evaporating area. Peering up, I see copper pipes that preheat the sap. Below is the evaporating pan with long shallow channels with gates and valves. The heat is oil. The exhaust fan above draws off the vapors. A thermostat keeps the syrup boiling at one hundred eighty to one hundred eighty-five degrees. Much higher than that and the syrup darkens.

We walk around the other side where a tap comes out of the bottom of the evaporator pan. The spigot empties into a metal cone perched in a pine frame and layered with filters. Two Orlon, one flannel, and a handful of paper ones that are removed one at a time as they fill with sugar sand.

Under the filter is a metal pail. When it is full it is carried across the room and emptied into a final holding tank.

Carmen and Robert tap more than two hundred trees, using a portable drill. They take in close to two hundred gallons of sap a day, and cook it down to syrup in about six hours. One year they got one hundred fifty-five gallons of syrup. One year they got sixteen. Usually they get around seventy.

They sell their syrup mostly, they say, to pay for the price of making it. Because they sell it they have to meet regulatory standards. The syrup must contain at least 66 percent sugar. At 67 percent it crystalizes in the jars. They try to bottle at 66.5.

Robert picks up a gizmo, a refractometer I'm told, from a steel table. It looks a little bit like a garlic press. He opens it, and squeezes a drop of syrup onto it from a dropper, then closes it, peers through an eyepiece, and hands it to me. I aim it toward the bare light bulb in the middle of the ceiling and put my eye to the opening. Inside is a calibrated scale, with a line through it. When the syrup is tested at sixty-eight degrees, the refractometer will tell the percentage of sugar in the sample.

They cite other numbers. The sweetness of the sap varies from year to year. Usually it's 2.7 percent, this year 3.2. Although Minnesota is not the biggest U.S. producer of maple syrup—that honor goes to Vermont—it does have the sweetest trees on the continent, according to Carl Vogt of the University of Minnesota. And sugar sand varies yearly as well.

There is no visible sugar sand in Carmen and Robert's syrup, nor is it the dark and brooding color of our Mud Lake trade kettle product. Robert picks up a USDA syrup grading kit. It consists of a wooden holder about six inches long with three sealed, two-inch-tall bottles in it, and space for a fourth. The first bottle has light-colored syrup, "Light Amber." The second is darker and is labeled "Medium Amber." The third, "Dark Amber," is darker yet.

Robert picks up a fourth bottle from the table with a sample of their syrup in it, and sets it in the rack next to Light Amber. It is almost a perfect match, and that is the grade that their labels will read.

I lean against a post in the middle of the sugar shack and Robert and Carmen and Douglas also find places to rest, and we continue our talk. The room we are in is utterly unlike the grove where Bill and I boil off. Its concrete floor and walls are scrubbed clean. There is no dust or dirt, no clutter. The equipment, even the sink in one corner, is made of institutional stainless steel. Only the filter bags and their wooden stand have texture.

Because the syrup is made in an enclosed system, the scent of sugar in the air is mild, not heavy and clinging as in our kitchen. But the conversation we have is the same as the ones I have with guests at home. We try to articulate the lure of this passion that is so incongruent with the age we live in.

"It's fun to see what you can produce," says Carmen, but there is more in her voice than that simple pleasure. She tells about the schoolchildren who come to visit, and send letters and drawings back in thanks. And she gives me newsletters and pamphlets from the syrup makers' association for which she is secretary.

And she adds to my list of homilies: "It's a good run the year after a drought," and "The sap is sweeter after a sunny year." But she and Robert are both skeptical about the value of wise sayings. "The only thing predictable about sugaring is that it is unpredictable," he says.

I tell them about the healthy tree I tapped that was dry no matter where I put the spile in. One day while I stood musing about it I looked up into the

Nate Wentworth gathers sap from one of two thousand taps in the Wildwood Farms sugarbush.

Nate, Nick, and Dustin Wentworth bring sap to a gathering tank in the sugarbush. The tank will be driven to the sugarhouse, several miles away.

The Wentworth family's Wildwood Farms commercial sugarhouse in northern Minnesota. Steam escaping from vents in the roof is from water evaporating off boiling sap.
Photos by Tamara Wentworth.

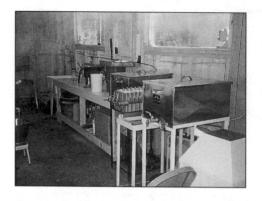

Commercial sugarers use special equipment to assure that their syrup complies with maple syrup industry standards. *Photo by Tamara Wentworth.*

crown of the tree as though I might find an answer there, and I did: a cluster of oak leaves dangling at the end of a branch.

We all laughed. There is always something to laugh about with sugaring, and the joke is usually on the sugarer. Still we turn ourselves over to the trees each spring, let them determine our days and nights, slog through snow and then muck to service them, all the while spending money and time and energy and hope.

I think about the other things some humans do by hand. Needlework, gardening, tying fishing flies. None makes sense in corporate terms. The bottom line lies in the heart.

When the Frogs Begin to Sing

LAST NIGHT THE FROGS began to sing. I heard them when I stepped outside for a few minutes to look at the stars. The bay and most of the swamp down the hill to the west are still frozen, but the little pond to the north of the driveway that dries up in August has been open for two days, and that is where the music came from. I listened to it for a few minutes and then went in and told Bill: Tomorrow will probably be our last day of sugaring.

Today I am out in the grove early, starting the ten gallons of sap we picked yesterday afternoon. The spiles were still dripping then, so there will be more, maybe another five gallons. Not enough for another day of boiling, so I'll add it to today's batch.

Bill usually gets the kettle going, but today he is doing other spring chores, and I will start and keep the fire.

I have done it before, and as with the cooking of the sap and the syrup, as I relearn the niceties of fire building, I remember them. I rummage in the plastic sack full of birch bark I gathered last fall from the house woodpile and find what I need. A half-dozen strips of papery bark, a few handfuls of medium-weight bark, and two or three heavier pieces, these last ones curled into tight, thick scrolls.

With a shovel I pull yesterday's ashes out to the edges of the fire pit and lay down a triangle of medium-sized sticks. These form a trivet that will allow air to flow under the fire. I nudge the papery strips of bark partway under the trivet, being careful to let some of their ends stick out like wicks, so I can reach them with matches. Then I set the medium and heavy bark on top of the trivet.

To build the rest of the fire I kneel in the soft, wet, and ashy dirt at the opening to the fire pit, scrunching my back down and bowing my head to the kettle. I am happy to stand up again to get twigs from the brush pile, and take a moment to stretch, shake out my arms, and to look around at the quiet morning.

It is good that this will be our last fire. The breezes and the sun have gathered most of the moisture from last year's grasses and leaves, and there is now danger of grass and forest fires. We have tramped a good buffer around the kettle, but ashes and sparks have wings, and burning in the open will probably be banned within a few days.

Breathing deeply of the sweet April air, I continue with my task. I place handfuls of small twigs on the birch bark, followed by handfuls of larger twigs, then small branches. I go to the bigger brush pile and pull out three long branches, diameters about two inches, and place the bigger ends into my pyramid. As the fire begins to work, I will feed these in, and will add others. Then I place a few small logs on top of it all, and pull the box of stick matches out of my pocket.

As I built the fire base, I kept my birch bark wicks in line, and now I ignite each one. The flames take immediately and do their job, finding their way under the kindling to ignite the heavier bark, which ignites the twigs, which ignite the branches, which ignite the logs. For half an hour I fuss and feed, shoving new branches into the base, and propping small, very dry or split logs on top of the collapsing structure. To make myself give the flames time to work, I adjust the skirt for the wind of the moment, and pick over the woodpiles for the right logs to add next.

Inside the kettle, the two gallons of sap we put there at the end of the last boiling off begins to hum and then sing. Bubbles scurry around the surface like water bugs. I bring over one of the holding pails from yesterday's pick and begin the gradual adding of the sap. I'll keep about five gallons in at a time, adding more as it boils off.

I have been outside for an hour. The fire is set now, the ever-renewing base of coals nibbling away at the wood I add. The sap is at a strong, silent simmer. I sit back in one of the lawn chairs amidst the sounds of this mid-April morning, five weeks after we drilled our test taps, and three weeks since we started cooking.

Most days I would go back in the house now and come out in a while, but the additional sap I'll pick and cook today will add hours to the task unless I keep up the fire. I don't mind. The air is mild. In the woods to the north, a phoebe is calling. In the tree behind me chickadees scrounge. The frogs are silent, but ducks that will share their water have come quacking in and are making ripples on the pond. A pair of bluebirds has chosen again to bless the birdhouse on the south edge of the sugarbush. Our three Salukis, no longer interested in our aberrant behavior, loll around on incipient grass and dream the sun into their bones.

I rouse myself from reverie, and fix the fire again, then go in the house for a short time, then return and add sap to the kettle and wood to the fire. On the tarp and outer logs of the heaped woodpile, spiders make webs. When I reach deep inside for a log I think I must have, I find ice.

Early in the afternoon, I check the spiles nearest the kettle. Though a few of the taps are moist, they are not running. Last night's light frost was not enough to swell the pressure in the trees. I take the remaining holding pails with yesterday's sap out of the cart, combine their contents into two instead of three, and set them near the kettle. I save out the two milk cans with covers, my favorites for picking, set them and one plastic pail in the cart, and start my rounds.

The first tree we tapped, the one closest to the driveway, one of the last to start running, does its best work toward the end of the season. Still, after moving from it to the one north, and then the one east, I have only a quart of sap. I cross the driveway back to the grove, empty the three pails closest to the kettle, pour all that I've picked into a plastic pail, and begin the trek through the fifteen trees east of the house and the two south.

I move slowly, watching out for the sapling balsams and the seedling maples, which are swelling with buds, and marveling at the chatter of the leaves disturbed by my feet. I check the north side of some trees. The tobacco I sprinkled there weeks ago, in thanks to the Ojibwe "grandfathers," is gone, has been received.

Most pails have from a cup to a quart of sap. Their liner bags are stiff and sticky from use, even though this is the second set of the season. And another of the cascade of spring harbingers is present: moths. They find their way into the bags even through the folds of the plastic. At almost every pail I release one or more, along with a fly or two.

The sap is not very good. It is not milky, but it is warmish, and dull. Even if we get good runs after this, we will not sugar. We'll pull the taps, and any sap that runs will water the tree, and birds and squirrels will stop for treats.

I return from the afternoon pick with the five gallons I anticipated, and resume my vigil at the fire. By dusk I have no sap left to keep up the five-gallon level in the kettle. Bill joins me for the finale. He tells me the pocket gophers are awake and are continuing their encroachment on my flower garden where tulips have breached into light and one daring anemone, two inches high, has opened a single blossom to the sun. And he has been to the lower garden: The rhubarb is surfacing.

We talk about pulling the taps, and wonder if it is safe yet to hook up the outside hose for washing the pails, or if we'll have more extended freezing. And we talk about the season's yield, eleven batches including this one, more than four gallons of syrup, enough for eating and for giving.

Bill understands the heat of the kettle better than I do, and he takes over the last of the fire, encouraging enough warmth to keep the sap reducing, but not so much that it will foam up and burn when it is time to take the incipient syrup into the house.

As the sugar content of the sap rises and Bill decreases the fire, the kettle again begins to sing, a quieter, softer song than the morning one when the sap is thin and full of water.

Tomorrow we return to the calendar. Our response to invitations will no longer be qualified by "it depends on the weather, on the sap run." We will still work outside, in our gardens, but at our leisure. Even tonight we feel the pull of the clock, and the empty pails hanging lightly on the spile hooks seem an anomaly. Spring has moved in.

To our left in the pond across the driveway, the frogs arouse and begin their song. To our right, in the kettle, the singing syrup harmonizes. Bill and I sit in between, in our sugarbush kitchen, and listen.

A Sugarer's
Library

THE MAPLE TREE

Approximately one hundred fifty species of the maple tree have been identified worldwide, mostly in the northern hemisphere. The great majority of them are native to eastern Asia, and many are found in Europe.

In spite of the global proliferation of maples, sugaring is essentially a North American activity. The five maples suitable for sugaring are indigenous to this continent, and do not appreciate being transplanted. In addition, to be even modestly successful, sugaring requires extended early-spring weather, with many weeks of temperatures that go below freezing at night and rise to about forty during the day. This precludes sugaring not only in places such as Scandinavia and Europe, where spring leaps quickly into summer, but in western Canada and the western and southern United States.

Of the twenty or so maple species now growing in the United States and Canada, about twelve are native. The others have been imported as ornamentals. Of the native trees, *Acer saccharum,* the sugar maple, is favored by sugarers, and is used almost exclusively by commercial operations. Its sap contains about 2 percent sugar. Next preferred is *Acer nigrum,* the black maple, with almost as high a sugar content.

The lesser cousins sometimes used for sugaring, usually by backyard sugarers, are *Acer saccharinum,* silver maple, and *Acer rubrum,* red maple. These contain about half the sugar of *A. saccharum* and *A. nigrum.* Another relative, *A. negundo,* the boxelder, the only maple with compound leaves, is also a favorite of backyarders. Although its sugar content is dismayingly small, it is a copious producer of sap, and its syrup is maple syrup.

Any maple tree that lives in the right place can be successfully tapped, but the right place means a clime with weather conditions that, during spring warm-up, cause atmospheric pressure inside the tree to exceed that of the pressure outside. When this occurs, sap will flow out through any aperture, including a broken stem, a hole nibbled by a squirrel, or one drilled by a human.

Other families of trees do have sugar in their sap, but not in as high a concentration as in the maple. One exception is the birch tree. Its sap is about as sweet as that of the boxelder, and syrup can be made by those willing to double or triple their cooking time. The sap of both birch and boxelder can be more efficiently used, however, in the making of beer or wine.

Maple trees can be tapped any time of the year when the temperature cooperates for a few days or more, including midwinter, and even in the fall. Midwinter tappings may be worth the effort, but fall tappings yield a sap that is considered by most to be undesirable in flavor and color.

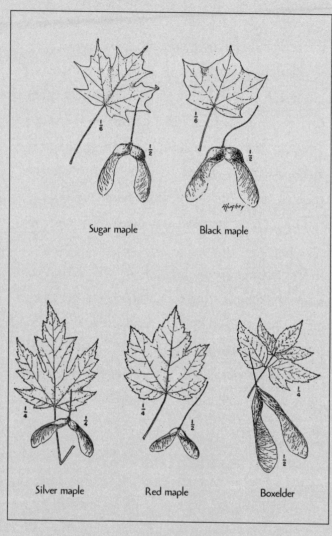

Sugar maple

Black maple

Silver maple

Red maple

Boxelder

Yearbook of Agriculture, 1949.

A BRIEF HISTORY
OF SUGARING

For as long as stories have been told, North Americans have captured sap from maple trees and coaxed it into syrup and then sugar. These rituals take place in the spring, in what is now known as the north central and northeastern United States, and southeastern Canada. While maple tree species abound in other areas of North America, and in other areas of the world, nowhere else do the three necessary weather factors collude to produce the internal pressure that allows maple sap to escape from the trees and into the buckets of the grateful human populace: winter dormancy; an early spring that is long and leisurely; and, during that season, temperatures that consistently rise above forty degrees Fahrenheit during the day and fall below freezing at night.

The first maple sap harvesters were the American Indians. When cooking the sap, they usually bypassed the syrup stage and went on to make sugar. The molten crystals were poured into molds, which made storage and transport easy. When the Indians wanted syrup, they added water to the sugar. The tasty, brown sugar and its syrup were used as both a spice and a sweetener.

American Indians traditionally tapped trees by making gouges in the bark. The sap was collected in troughs. Two methods of reducing the sap were used. The water was either boiled off over a fire in clay, bark, or wood pots, or frozen off. The ice in a partially frozen container of sap did not contain sugar, and so was cast off. This process could be repeated until only syrup remained.

European settlers were quick to learn sugar making from the Indians. Over time, in exchange they offered new ways to expedite the process. Copper and iron kettles replaced the indigenous cooking pots. To release the sap from the trees, instead of gouges and troughs, augers were used to drill tap holes into which spiles were placed. Wooden and then metal buckets took the place of birch bark baskets for gathering sap.

There was one aspect of sugaring that these early European accoutrements did not change: For the lack of suitable containers, the European settlers followed the Indian practice of making sugar instead of syrup. It was not until the Civil War, with the invention of the tin can, that maple syrup became a popular product.

Well into the 1800s, maple sugar was the only sugar readily available to North Americans. However, in the late 1800s, the cane sugar industry in the Caribbean began to compete with the homemade delicacy. After a war that included tariffs on the refined, tasteless white sugar, and bounties for maple sugar production, maple sugar gave way to the mass-production economy of cane sugar. During the first half of the twentieth century, except for brief periods during World War I and World War II, when maple sugar helped ease the North American sugar shortage, maple sugar and its companion, maple syrup, became delicacies valued for their flavor rather than for their sweetening power.

Today, maple syrup, not sugar, is the favored maple product. Nearly seven million gallons are produced annually in North America. In Canada, most maple syrup is produced commercially in Quebec. In the United States, with Vermont leading the way, maple syrup is also produced commercially in New York, Maine, Wisconsin, Pennsylvania, New Hampshire, and Michigan, in that order.

KEEPING SUGARING
RECORDS

I t is a good idea to keep records of your sugaring
efforts. Even if you tap only one or two trees, you
will want to know the ratio of sap to syrup, and the
dates when you sugared. Here's a sample of one
year from our sugaring logs, and our summary log
for all years.

SUGARING LOG: 1994

BATCH	DATE	APPROXIMATE GALLONS OF SAP	PINTS OF SYRUP
I	March 21	10	2.75
II	March 22	10	2.25
III	March 23–27	17	4.50
IV	March 31	17	4.25
V	April 1	10	2.50
VI	April 5	22	6.00
VII	April 7	13	3.50
VIII	April 9	10	3.00
IX	April 10	10	3.50
X	April 11	10	3.00
XI	April 12	18	5.00
		147 gallons	40.25 (= 5 gallons)

Sugaring Log: Yearly Totals

YEAR	DATES	# DAYS IN SEASON	# TAPS
1984	March 25–April 6	13	19
1985	March 9–April 18	40	22
1986	April 1–April 16	16	8
1987	March 6–March 23	17	19
1988	March 17–April 26	40	19
1989	March 30–April 21	21	15
1990–1993	Drought; lassitude		
1994	March 16–April 12	30	20
1996	April 6–May 5	16	18

Note: Our ratio is approximately 30 to 1, better than the average 40 to 1, but not unusual in Minnesota.

# BATCHES	APPROXIMATE GALLONS OF SAP	PINTS/GALLONS OF SYRUP
xi	120	32/4
xxii	258	69/8.6
vii	?	14/1.75
ii	30	8/1
ix	112.5	30/3.75
xii	?	40/5
xi	150	40/5
viii	lost count	50/6.25

A SUGARER'S BOOKSHELF

My first sugaring book was *The Maple Sugar Book* (Schocken Books, 1979, now out of print, but available at some libraries) by back-to-the-land gurus Helen and Scott Nearing. It's both a history and a how-to book, and I got tired just reading it, so it was good preparation for our own sugaring experience. My most recent sugaring book is *Sweet Maple: Life, Lore and Recipes from the Sugarbush* (Lawrence & Martin, Chapters Publishing, 1993). It speaks clearly and thoroughly about the history, lore, science, and practice of sugaring, and is beautifully illustrated.

Most of my other information comes from chapters or entries in books with a broader subject. My favorites are Euell Gibbons' *Stalking the Wild Asparagus* (Alan C. Hood & Company, 1987) and Noel Perrin's *First Person Rural* (Godine, 1978). I also rely heavily on pamphlets from state agriculture and natural-resource departments, booklets from the United States Department of Agriculture Forest

Service, and magazine articles (often listed in the *Reader's Guide to Periodical Literature*).

For homespun how-to, Noel Perrin's *Amateur Sugar Maker* (University Press of New England, 1992) captures the casual nature of home sugaring, as does Rink Mann's *Backyard Sugarin'* (The Countryman Press, 1976). Home how-to help, commercial operation information, and supply house lists are also available from state sugaring associations, the North American Maple Council, and the International Maple Syrup Institute. Current addresses for these organizations are usually available from departments of agriculture and natural resources in states where maple sap is harvested.